The Complete Guide on How to Knit from Beginner to Expert

Learn How to Knit from Beginner to Expert

Basic Knitting Techniques and Stitches for Beginners

By Dorothy Wilks

Thank you for purchasing this book on learning how to knit. Knitting is an art form and in this book we'll learn the basic stitches and techniques you need to know to start your love affair with this craft. We will learn all about yarn and the different fibers available, the basic equipment you'll need to start out, basic stitches and techniques, and how to read a knitting pattern. My mother was an avid knitter and I grew up watching her create many beautiful projects including intricate sweaters for my father and I. This book is geared for the absolute beginner, but if you need to brush up on your basic skills you'll find it useful as well. So are you ready to begin your knitting journey? I am so let's go!

Contents

Equipment for Beginners

As a beginning knitter you will need some basic equipment to start out. Of course you'll need knitting needles and a pair of shears. You will also need stitch markers, a row counter, and a container to store your yarn, projects, and equipment. We'll go over all these things in this chapter and learn about the different types of needles and the accessories you can purchase to help you start out on the right foot. Right now don't spend a fortune on equipment. Buy good quality equipment, but a nice set of aluminum knitting needles will serve you for many years. The most common sizes called for are size 8 and 10; so if you want to purchase separate sets of knitting needles those two sizes will serve you well.

Knitting Needle Sizes

Knitting needles come in a wide variety of sizes and lengths. Most needles are listed in US sizing, but you may find patterns or needles which use a different scale of measurement.

US	UK	Imperial
4		3.5
5	9	3.75
6		4.25
7	7	4.5
8	6	5.0
9	5	5.5
10	4	6.0
10.5	3	6.50
11	0	8.0
13	00	9.0
15	000	10.0
17	0000	13.0
19	00000	15.0
35		19.0

Straight Knitting Needles

Straight needles come in sets of two and have a pointed end and an end with a knot on it. Stitches are moved from one needle to the other as you work. Straight needles come in a wide variety of sizes from very small needles used for lace to large needles used with bulky yarn. They also come in different lengths to accommodate different sized projects. A pair of size 8 and size 10, 10 to 14 inch straight needles is a good investment for the beginner.

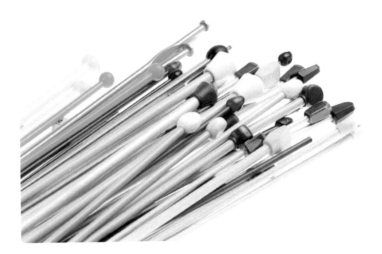

Circular Knitting Needles

Circular knitting needles are two needles joined by a length of metal or plastic. As you knit the stitches rest on the length between the two needles. This enables you to work in the round or on large projects. You rarely turn your work when knitting with circular needles like you do with straight needles. Circular needles come in the same needles sizes as straight needles, as well as different lengths. If you are going to knit a hat you would need shorter circular needles than if you were to knit a large afghan.

Double Point Needles

As the name implies double point needles have points on each end. They come in sets of four, five, or six and are used to knit small projects in the round. One double point needle is always the working needle with the stitches distributed evenly around the other needles. As you work the stitches are moved from one needle to the next and you work around and around. You usually don't turn your work with knitting with double point needles.

Cable Needles

Cable needles are used to hold stitches when creating cables. Cable knitting is fun and easier than it sounds. As you knit you slip stitches onto the cable needle and hold them either in the front or back of your work and then knit them off the cable needle. This produces the very lovely cables you see in many knitting projects. Cable needles can either be straight, curved, or large hooks. In my opinion a curved or hooked cable needle is best for the beginning knitter since the stitches are held more securely than on straight cable needles. Cable needles are usually sold in sets.

Stitch Markers

Stitch markers are used to mark the beginning of a round, the beginning and ending of a pattern repeat, and to help keep track of where you are in a pattern. They come in many different styles from simple round plastic rings to intricate ones with beads and decorations. Round stitch markers are slipped from needle to needle as you work and normally used within a row. Clip on stitch markers are also easy to use and you can clip them on and off to move them as you work.

Row Counter

A row counter is a handy little tool to have in your toolbox. They help you keep track of what row you're working on and can be as simple as a piece of paper and pencil to hand held clickers. When you start to work a pattern it is essential for you to know what row you're on so you can keep track of your progress. I recommend getting into the habit of using a row counter as you knit from the very start.

Shears

One of the most important tools you will need is a good quality pair of shears (scissors). These should only be used to cut yarn, thread, and fabric so that they stay sharp. Make sure your family knows they are off limits especially when they need to cut paper. Paper will dull your shears and make them a nightmare to use when cutting yarn.

Storage

You will also need something to store your equipment, yarn, and works in progress. Depending on your situation you may just need a large bag, but if you're me and have pets, or if you have small curious children, you will need something that will keep your things safe. I use a large plastic bin with a lid that snaps shut. This keeps my cats from getting into my yarn and dragging it around the house. One of my cats will just get in there and sleep, but one of my little darlings has a bad habit of trying to get in my bin and dig and root around. You can imagine the mess this makes! As your yarn stash grows you may want to invest in more tubs or get some attractive shelves to store your yarn in.

Yarn and Yarn Fibers

Welcome to the world of yarn! Yarn comes in many different colors, textures, weights, and types. I will warn you, you will probably develop a love of yarn that may challenge your budget. My family teases me about scouring the internet for yarn sales and how excited I get when my latest acquisitions arrive. Ignore the haters and revel in your new love of yarn! Okay seriously, yarn is cool.

In this chapter we'll learn about the basic fibers used to create yarn, how yarn is made, how to read a yarn label, and I'll share some tips on how to pick the perfect yarn for your knitting projects.

Yarn Weights

Yarn comes in weights from lace and fingerling (0) to very bulky (6). Each weight is suitable for different types of projects. Lace and fingerling yarn is very thin and creates a delicate looking fabric while super bulky and bulky yarn is very thick and works up very quickly. The most common weights used are 3 and 4. This chart from the Craft Yarn Council is a handy guide to help you understand the different yarn weights.

Yarn Weight Symbol & Category Names	LACE 0 DENTELLE Liston	SUPER FINE 1 SUPER FIN Super Fino	FINE 2 FIN Fino	LIGHT 3 LEGER Ligero	MEDIUM 4 MOYEN Medio	BULKY 5 BULKY Abultado	SUPER BULKY 6 TRES ÉPAIS Super Abultado
Type of Yarns in Category	Fingering 10-count crochet thread	Sock, Fingerling, Baby	Sport, Baby	DK, Light Worsted	Worsted, Afghan, Aran	Chunky, Craft, Rug	Bulky, Roving
Knit Gauge Range* in Stockinette Stitch to 4 inches	33–40** sts	27–32 sts	23–26 sts	21–24 st	16–20 sts	12–15 sts	6–11 sts
Recommended Needle in Metric Size Range	1.5–2.25 mm	2.25—3.25 mm	3.25—3.75 mm	3.75—4.5 mm	4.5—5.5 mm	5.5—8 mm	8 mm and larger
Recommended Needle U.S. Size Range	000–1	1 to 3	3 to 5	5 to 7	7 to 9	9 to 11	11 and larger

Yarn Fibers

Yarn is created from three basic types of fibers; animal, plant, and synthetic. Animal yarn includes wool, alpaca, cashmere and angora. The fibers are taken from the wool or fur of these animals, spun into yarn fibers, and then these fibers are dyed and spun into yarn.

Merino Rams

Animal Fibers

Wool is a very versatile fiber and is a good choice for the beginning knitter. Wool blended with acrylic produces a warm spongy fabric which is easy to care for. Wool yarn is strong and needs to be blocked after being hand washed.

Alpaca yarn is also very versatile and produces a nice warm fabric. Alpaca has good drape and is has more shine than wool. Mohair is from goats and dyed into very vibrant colors. Alpaca and mohair also must be hand washed and blocked.

Cashmere and angora are very luxurious and expensive yarns. They produce ultra-soft fabrics and need special care. Almost all animal fiber yarns must be hand washed, washed on the gentle cycle in a machine, and are never dried in a dryer.

Plant Fibers

Yarn is also made from various plant fibers. These include cotton, linen, bamboo, and hemp. Plant based yarns are lightweight and strong. They give you a very pretty stitch definition and are perfect for warm weather accessories and garments. Plant fiber yarn may be machine washed and dried, or they may need to be hand washed and blocked. Be sure to check the yarn label for the appropriate care instructions.

Cotton

Cotton yarn is spun from the fibers of the cotton bole (the puffy white part of the plant). These boles are picked, combed and cleaned, and then the fibers are spun and dyed into cotton yarn. Cotton yarn absorbs moisture very well so it is the top choice for kitchen and bath projects. You can find cotton yarn in many different weights and colors.

Linen

Linen yarn is made from the fibers of the flax plant. The flax plant fibers are cleaned, spun, and dyed into vibrant yarn which is great for use in summer garments. Linen knit fabric breaths and wicks away moisture to keep you cool in warm weather.

Bamboo

Bamboo yarn is very similar to cotton, but it has a bit more give and sheen. It gives very pretty stitch definition and is lovely when used for lacy garments and shawls. Bamboo is one of my favorite yarns to work with, but for the beginner it can be a bit slick to work with until you get used to it.

Hemp

Hemp is also very similar to cotton, but produces a super sturdy fabric which is great for rugs and other accessories. The same fibers used to make hemp ropes are spun and refined to make hemp yarn. Hemp yarn usually comes in natural and neutral colors and is suitable for lots of projects.

Synthetic Fibers

One of the most popular types of yarn is acrylic yarn. This yarn is produced from petroleum fibers and sup into many different weights, colors, and textures. Acrylic yarn is the perfect yarn for the beginner because it is easy to work with, easy to care for, and comes in almost any weight and color you can imagine. Acrylic yarn can be machine washed and dried and normally does not need to be blocked to retain its shape. Popular brands of acrylic yarn include Red Heart Super Saver, Caron Soft, and Lion Brand Heartland.

Other synthetic fibers may be blended into animal, plant or other synthetic yarns to add sheen, texture, and stretch. These include microfiber and polyester.

Balls, Skeins, and Hanks

Most yarn comes in skeins or balls. Balls are made to be pulled from the outside while a skein is made to be pulled from the center. Hanks are not to be used without being rolled into a ball. If you try use a hank without first rolling it into a ball first. Otherwise you will have a giant mess on your hands. I would recommend you invest in a nice medium priced yarn winders and swift. The swift adjust and holds the yarn while the ball winder does just what the name implies, it rolls the yarn into a ball. You might want to roll all of your yarn into balls to be sure there are no breaks or knots in it.

Place the yarn on the swift and adjust it so that the yarn sits securely but not too tight, or too loose. Next thread the ball winder according to the manufacturer's instructions and slowly wind the yarn up into a ball or a cake. You can find electric ball winders or manual ones depending on your budget. Keep the tension even and wind slowly so that no knots or tangles form. Once you're done you have a nice even and uniform ball of yarn to work with.

How to Read a Yarn Label

A yarn label has all the information you need to choose the correct yarn for your project. On the label you will find the fiber content, the weight, the suggested needle size, and how to care for the fabric once your project is knitted. Understanding how to read a yarn label is essential for the beginner and for any level of knitter.

This chart from Lion Brand Yarn shows the most common care symbols used on today's yarn labels.

Machine Wash, Normal	Do Not Wash	Tumble Dry, Permanent Press
Machine Wash, Cold	Dryclean	Tumble Dry, Gentle
Machine Wash, Cold	Dryclean, Any Solvent	Do Not Tumble Dry
Machine Wash, Warm	Dryclean, Petroleum Solvent Only	Do Not Dry
Machine Wash, Warm	Dryclean, Any Solvent Except Trichloroethylene	Line Dry
Machine Wash, Hot	Dryclean, Short Cycle	Drip Dry
Machine Wash, Hot	Dryclean, Reduced Moisture	Dry Flat
Machine Wash, Hot	Dryclean, Low Heat	Dry In Shade
Machine Wash, Hot	Dryclean, No Steam	Do Not Wring
Machine Wash, Hot	Do Not Dryclean	Iron, Any Temperature, Steam or Dry
Machine Wash, Hot	Bleach When Needed	Iron, Low
Machine Wash, Hot	Non-Chlorine Bleach When Needed	Iron, Medium

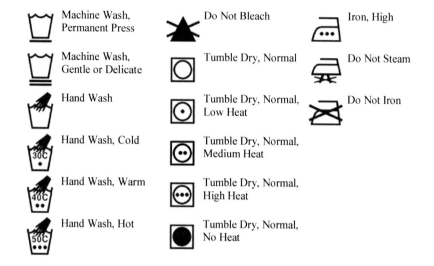

	Machine Wash, Permanent Press		Do Not Bleach		Iron, High
	Machine Wash, Gentle or Delicate		Tumble Dry, Normal		Do Not Steam
	Hand Wash		Tumble Dry, Normal, Low Heat		Do Not Iron
	Hand Wash, Cold		Tumble Dry, Normal, Medium Heat		
	Hand Wash, Warm		Tumble Dry, Normal, High Heat		
	Hand Wash, Hot		Tumble Dry, Normal, No Heat		

In this example of common yarn label you can see the yarn is a medium size 4 yarn and a size US 8 knitting needle is recommended. The fabric knitted with this yarn can be machine washed in water no hotter than 104 degrees, and it can be tumble dried on low. So this would be a good choice for a beginning knitting project.

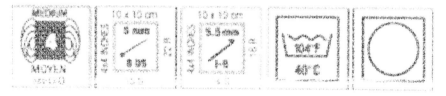

Gauge

One of the most important pieces of information on a yarn label is the gauge. Gauge refers to how many stitches and rows it takes to knit a four inch by four inch piece of fabric using the recommended needle size. In this example if you used a US size 8 knitting needle a row of 15 stitches and 22 rows should create a four inch square gauge swatch.

If your swatch is too large tighten up your tension or go down a needle size. If your swatch it too small you maybe knitting too tightly or you may need to use a larger needle. Always make a gauge swatch before you begin your project. This will save you lots of headaches later and is a good practice to get into.

How to Read a Written Knitting Pattern

I see people on the knitting groups I belong to say they can't read patterns. Being able to read patterns is an important skill to develop. Patterns aren't really hard once you understand all the information to be found in them. Once you get the knack of reading patterns an entire new world of possibilities opens up to you.

Standard Abbreviations

Most designers use a standardized set of abbreviations in their patterns. This chart is from the Craft Yarn Council and can be used with most patterns you will find in print and online today.

Abbreviation	Description	Abbreviation	Description
[ ]	work instructions within brackets as many times as directed	pat(s) or patt	pattern(s)
( )	work instructions within parentheses in the place directed	pm	place marker
* *	repeat instructions following the asterisks as directed	pop	popcorn
*	repeat instructions following the single asterisk as directed	p2tog	purl 2 stitches together
"	inch(es)	prev	previous
alt	alternate	psso	pass slipped stitch over
approx	approximately	pwise	purlwise
beg	begin/beginning	rem	remain/remaining
bet	between	rep	repeat(s)
BO	bind off	rev St st	reverse stockinette stitch
CA	color A	RH	right hand

CB	color B	**rnd(s)**	round(s)
CC	contrasting color	**RS**	right side
cm	centimeter(s)	sk	skip
cn	cable needle	**skp**	slip, knit, pass stitch over— one stitch decreased
CO	cast on	**sk2p**	slip 1, knit 2 together, pass slip stitch over the knit 2 together; 2 stitches have been decreased
cont	continue	**sl**	slip
dec	decrease/ decreases/ decreasing	**sl1k**	slip 1 knitwise
dpn	double pointed needle(s)	**sl1p**	slip 1 purlwise
fl	front loop(s)	**sl st**	slip stitch(es)
foll	follow/follows/ following	ss	slip stitch (Canadian)
g	gram	**ssk**	slip, slip, knit these 2 stiches together—a decrease
inc	increase/increases/ increasing	sssk	slip, slip, slip, knit 3 stitches together
k or **K**	knit	**st(s)**	stitch(es)
k2tog	knit 2 stitches together	**St st**	stockinette stitch/stocking stitch
kwise	knitwise	**tbl**	through back loop
LH	left hand	**tog**	together

lp(s)	loop(s)	**WS**	wrong side
m	meter(s)	**wyib**	with yarn in back
M1	make one stitch	**wyif**	with yarn in front
M1 p-st	make one purl stitch	**yd(s)**	yard(s)
MC	main color	**yfwd**	yarn forward
mm	millimeter(s)	**yo**	yarn over
oz	ounce(s)	yrn	yarn around needle
p or P	purl	yon	yarn over needle

As a beginner you won't see all of these abbreviations in the patterns you will knit, but it is good to have this chart to refer to as you advance in your skills. You can find the link to this chart in the back of this book if you want to visit the website and print it out for reference.

Reading an Actual Pattern

Now we're going to learn how to read an actual pattern. First look for the skill level, what supplies and yarn you need, and if there are any special stitches you need to know to knit the project. For our example we'll be looking at a free Red Heart pattern designed by Trish Warrick called Funtastic Scarf.

LW2888

BEGINNER

knitting
Design by Trish Warrick

What you will need:

RED HEART® Gumdrop™: 1 ball each of 930 Orange A and 620 Cherry B.

Susan Bates® Knitting Needles: 5 mm [US 8].

You can see this is a beginner pattern and you will need one skein of Red Heart Gumdrop yarn in each color of Orange and Cherry. You will also need a pair of US size 8 knitting needles.

GAUGE: 22 sts = 4" (10 cm), 19 rows = 4" (10 cm) in pattern. CHECK YOUR GAUGE. Use any size needles to obtain the gauge.

The gauge for the scarf is 22 stitches and 19 rows equal a four inch gauge swatch. Be sure to make a gauge swatch to check your tension and if you are using the correct size of needles.

ABBREVIATIONS
K = knit; mm = millimeter; P = purl; st(s) = stitch(es); [ ] = work directions in brackets as indicated.

Always check the abbreviations used for each pattern you knit. Although most designers used standardized abbreviations, they may also use abbreviations which are unique to their particular pattern. In this pattern you see the abbreviations are pretty straight forward.

K equals knit

Mm equals millimeter

P equals purl

St(s) equals stitch or stitches

Instructions in parenthesis indicate pattern repeats. You will work the stitches inside the parenthesis as many times as indicated.

Finished Size: 4" (10 cm) wide x 40" (102 cm) long.

The pattern will also give you the finished dimensions of your project.

Once you know the amount and type of yarn you need, the size of needles, the specific abbreviations used in the pattern, the gauge, and the finished dimensions you are ready to get into the actual pattern.

First cast on 22 stitches with Color A. Knit rows 1-12 with Color A. Rows 13 – 27 are knitted with Color B, and the remaining rows are knitted with Color A. Once you reach the end bind off and weave in the ends.

Row 1 is knitted with knit 2 stitches, a pattern repeat starts and is purl 2 and knit 2. You repeat this across the row to the end. Read each row noting the stitches in parenthesis as being pattern repeats.

SCARF
With A, cast on 22 sts.

Row 1: K2, [P2, K2] across.

Row 2: K1, [P2, K2] across to last st, K1.

Row 3: K2, [P2, K2] across.

Row 4: K3, P2,[K2, P2] across to last st, K1.

Row 5: K2, [P2, K2] across.

Row 6: K1, [P2, K2] across to last st, K1.

Row 7: K2, [P2, K2] across.

Row 8: K3, P2,[K2, P2] across to last st, K1.

Row 9: K2, [P2, K2] across.

Row 10: K1, [P2, K2] across to last st, K1.

Row 11: K2, [P2, K2] across.

Row 12: K3, P2,[K2, P2] across to last st, K1; drop A.

Rows 13 and 14: With B, knit across.
Repeat Rows 1-14 for pattern until Scarf measures approximately 37½" (95 cm); then repeat Rows 1-12 once more.

Bind off all sts in pattern.

And here is the pretty finished product!

Basic Knitting Stitches and Techniques

We have covered the equipment you need, learned about yarn, and how to read a pattern. Now we're ready to pick up a pair of knitting needles and learn how to knit! In this chapter I will teach you the basic stitches you need to begin knitting beginner and easy patterns.

All knitting is a combination of knit and purl stitches. No matter how complicated a pattern or stitch may be they can all be broken down to these two basic stitches.

Casting On

Before you can knit your first stitch you must first get the yarn on your needles. This process is known as casting on. Remember that your cast on is not counted as the first row in a pattern. In this section we will learn the long tail casting method and the knit on casting method.

Long Tail Cast On

With the long tail cast on method you use the tail of the yarn to create the cast on stitches. If you're unsure how much yarn you will need cast on about an inch of stitches, unravel them and then multiply the amount of yarn you used to make up the correct measurement of your project.

First make a slip knot and place it on your knitting needle.

Hold the yarn from the skein and the tail in the palm of your left hand. Place your thumb and forefinger between the two pieces of yarn pull the knitting needle down and and pull up on the yarn to form "bunny ears". Take the needle and slip it under the yarn around your thumb, up under the yarn held by your forefinger, and back through the loop on your thumb. This forms a cast on stitch. Continue to do this until you have the appropriate number of stitches on your needle.

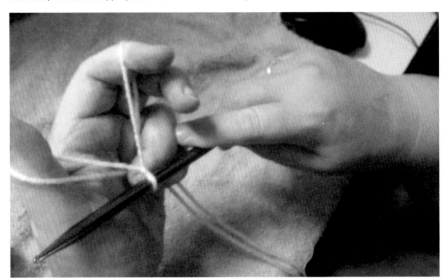

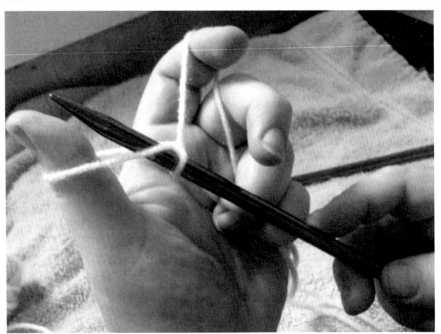

Knitting On Cast Method

The knit on casting method works just as the name sounds. You knit new stitches onto the needle. First place a slip knot onto the left needle. Place the right needle under the yarn as if to knit and yarn over. Pull the yarn through the stitch on your needle, but don't let the stitch come off the left needle. Place the tip of the right needle up under the stitch on the right needle and slip it back onto the left needle. Continue until you have the correct number of cast on stitches.

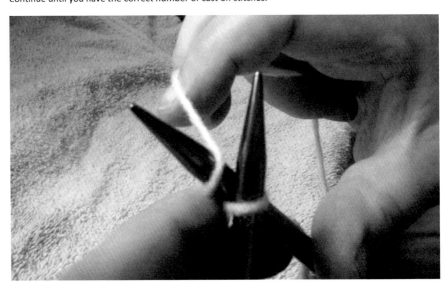

Knit Stitch

Once you have all of your stitches cast on you're ready to start knitting. The knit stitch is created by slipping the tip of the right needle through the first stitch on the left needle from the back. The working yarn is held in the back of your work while you knit. Wrap the yarn around the right needle from front to back and slip the stitch off the left needle. When you are ready to purl you will need to pull the yarn to the front of your work.

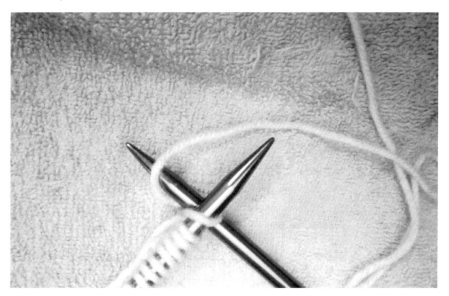

Purl Stitch

The purl stitch is knitted by pulling the working yarn to the front of your work and inserting the right needle into the stitch on the left needle from the front. Wrap the yarn over the right needle from the back to the front and slip the stitch off the left needle. When you are ready to go back to knit stitches pull the yarn to the back of the work.

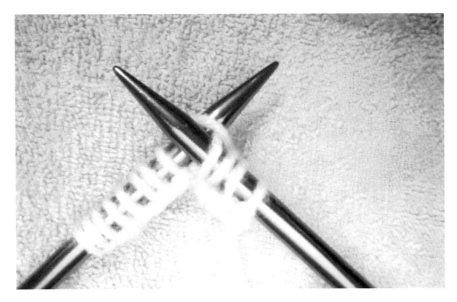

Slip Stitch

Slip stitches are just like knit and purl, but you do not wrap the yarn. Simply insert the right needle either knitwise (like you were going to knit) or purlwise (like you were going to purl) into the stitch on the left needle and slip the stitch onto the right needle.

Casting Off

Once you have completed all of your rows you'll need to get the fabric off the needles. This is known as casting off. You can cast off with knit or purl stitches. If you are using knit stitches knit two stitches. Take the left needle and slip it under the first knit stitch and pull it over the second stitch and let it drop off the needles. Knit another stitch, slip the left needle into the first stitch, slip it over the second stitch and let it drop off the needles. Continue in this manner until you get to the last two stitches. After you cast off the next to last stitch remove the needle and pull the yarn up through the stitch. Cut the yarn leaving a long tail to weave in and pull the tail through the last stitch.

Increases

There will be times in a pattern when you need to increase the number of stitches in a row. This is known as an increase. To knit or purl and increase look at the loop between the stitch you just worked and the next one on the left needle. This loop is where you need to insert the right needle to knit or purl a stitch. This increases the stitch count by one.

Decreases

You will also need to decrease stitches from time to time in a pattern. This is easily done by inserting the right needle into two stitches at once and either knitting or purling them. This reduces the stitch count in the row by one.

Knitting in the Round

When knitting in the round you will need to join the cast on stitches to form a circle. You can simply join them by knitting or purling the first and last stitch together making sure you don't twist the stitches. Or you can use a slip stitch to join. To use this method cast on one extra stitch. Slip the first stitch onto the right needle and slip the next onto the right needle. Place the left needle under the first slip stitch and pull it over the second slip stitch and pull the yarn up gently to secure. Now you can place a stitch marker and start to knit in the round.

Changing Colors

One of the fun things about knitting is the use of color. Changing colors is not hard in knitting. All you do is pick up the new color and start to knit with it. If you are changing colors at the beginning of a row use both the tail and the working end of the yarn to knit with for a few stitches. (Just be sure when you go across the row you knit with both loops so you don't create increases.) You can also catch the old color in the first stitch of the new color to secure it. The first stitch will feel a bit loose, but if you snug up the yarns it will be secure. This method works no matter if you are on the beginning of a row or in the middle. Be sure to leave a long tail so you can weave it in later.

Weaving in Tails

You must weave in the tails of your yarn. If you don't the yarn will work its way loose and your work will become undone. The best method I've found is to thread a tapestry needle with the tail and weave the tail in and out of the stitches for about an inch, turn your work and weave it for another inch, and then turn your work a third time and weave the tail in and out again. Work in and out of the loops of the fabric and once you've turned directions at least three times you can then trim the tail.

Blocking Knitted Fabric

Many knitted projects look and fit better if they are blocked. Blocking relaxes the fibers and lets the stitch work really shine through. Check the care instructions of the yarn and follow these to gently wash it. You can also dampen the yarn with a spray bottle of water. Roll the fabric up in a big towel to remove the excess moisture.

Now on a flat surface spread out either a couple of very thick towels or blocking squares. Flatten and shape the project with your hands first and then use dressmaker or blocking pins to pin the edges of the fabric gently pulling the fabric taut so that it is the correct shape. Once you have the fabric blocked let it dry completely before you remove it from the towels or blocking squares. You can see in the following images how much blocking adds to the beauty of the shawl.

Shawl before blocking

Shawl after blocking

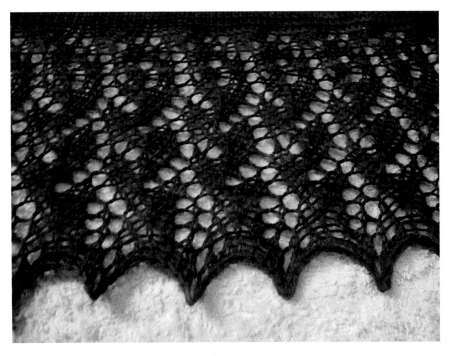

Close up of edging after blocking

These are the basic stitches and techniques you need to get started in knitting. I have shared some great video links at the end of this book to help you learn even more. You can find hundreds of free beginner patterns at the major yarn sites such as Red Heart, Lion Brand Yarn, and Yarnspirations. Be sure to check out the many groups on Facebook dedicated to knitting and join in the social media fun.

I hope this book has inspired you to try your hand at knitting. It is a craft and a hobby that will keep you busy for hours and help you create treasured projects for your family and friends.

Attributions

All images shared from Flickr are shared under the Creative Commons License.

Standard Yarn Weight System
http://www.craftyarncouncil.com/weight.html
Source: Craft Yarn Council

Yarn Winder
https://www.flickr.com/photos/stevier/3502590877
image shared on Flickr by Stevie Rocco

Yarn Label Chart
http://www.lionbrand.com/yarnCare.html
Source: Lion Brand Yarn

Yarn Label
www.craftyarncouncil.com/label.html
Source: Craft Yarn Council

Knitting Abbreviations Master List
http://www.craftyarncouncil.com/knit.html
Source: Craft Yarn Council

Funtastic Scarf Images
http://www.redheart.com/free-patterns/funtastic-scarf
Source: Red Heart

Shawl Before Blocking
https://www.flickr.com/photos/lacuna007/3933120280
Image shared on Flickr by Andrea Black

Shawl After Blocking
https://www.flickr.com/photos/lacuna007/3932339493
Image shared on Flickr by Andrea Black

Close Up of Edging on Shawl After Blocking
https://www.flickr.com/photos/lacuna007/3933121230
Image shared on Flickr by Andrea Black

Videos

How to Knit Series
https://www.youtube.com/watch?v=ONVQCK_-rKc
Expression Fiber Arts

How to Cast On
http://newstitchaday.com/?s=cast+on
New Stitch a Day

How to Knit the Invisible Join
http://newstitchaday.com/how-to-knit-the-invisible-join-in-the-round/
New Stitch a Day

How to Change Colors
http://newstitchaday.com/change-yarn-color/
New Stitch a Day

Book 2

Learn How to Knit Volume 2

Intermediate Knitting Techniques to Expand Your Skills

By Dorothy Wilks

Thank you for purchasing the second volume of my Learn How to Knit series. In this book we will learn how to read knitting graphs and explore some fun ways to use color in knitting. We will also learn intermediate knitting techniques such as creating beautiful cables which add texture and beauty to your knitting projects and how to cut knitted fabric safely. This book is geared toward the knitter that has learned the basics and would like to take the next step in this popular art form. So if you're ready gather up your needles and yarn and let's get started!

Contents

How to Read Knitting Graphs

Knitting graphs are visual representations of a knitting pattern. Instead of many lines of written out instructions a graph is an easy way to share a complicated pattern. When you can read knitting graphs you open up an entire new world of pattern possibilities. You may even want to create your own knitting graphs so you can personalize your projects for family and friends.

Now I know what you're thinking, a graph?? Oh my…but relax we're going to take this one step at a time and by the time we finish with this chapter you'll be able to work a basic graph and understand how graphs are written and how to use them.

First let's take a look at a basic graph. In this heart graph you can see there are 12 columns and 10 rows. Each square in a row represents a knit or purl stitch so that the finished square will have 10 rows with 12 stitches in each row.

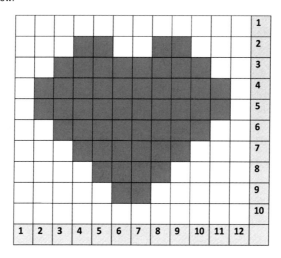

Most designers number the rows and stitches across to make it easier for you to keep track of where you are in a graph, but not all do. If there are no numbers you may want to jot them down on the side of the graph to help you track your progress.

Also look for a key to reading the graph. While most graphs just use colors to denote the pattern, some designers may use symbols to denote color and the type of stitch you need to use. For this example we will be working in the simple stockinette stitch (knit one row, purl one row).

To begin cast on 12 stitches. Since we'll be flat knitting we'll be turning our work at the end of each row. Start reading the graph on the lower right hand corner and knit the first row across in all white. Turn your work and now start reading the graph on the second row starting on the left hand side and purl this row working 5 white stitches, 2 red, and then 5 more in white. Turn your work, read the third row from right to left and knit 4 white stitches, 4 red stitches, and 4 white stitches. Continue to turn your work reading the odd rows from right to left, and the even rows from left to right changing colors as indicated.

If you were to work in the round you would not be turning your work so you would read all of the rows from right to left. When you come to the end of a row you would go back to the right side of the graph and read the next row and knit it as indicated with the appropriate color changes.

That really is all there is to reading a graph.

Tips for Working with Knitting Graphs

Take your time and take a deep breath. Some charts, like Fair Isle, can be a bit intimidating when you first look at them. But if you go row by row the graph will make more sense.

Know the color technique you will be using before you begin. Intarsia and Fair Isle use different types of techniques and some graphs as more suited to each type of color work. Intarsia graphs are usually fairly simple with only a few colors while Fair Isle graphs can use many different colors and have several color changes in a row.

Look at the graph carefully and make sure you know how many colors you will need before you begin. Familiarize yourself with the pattern and stitches needed before you begin.

Use a ruler, highlighter, or sticky note to keep track of what row you are on. Highlight each row as you complete it, and you may want to draw an arrow on a sticky note and move it up the graph to help you remember which way you need to read the next row.

Take your time and don't let a large graph intimidate you. Take the graph one row at a time. This will help you focus on the row at hand and not feel like you are taking on more than you can handle. Most of all have fun!

Intarsia Color Technique

Intarsia knitting creates pictures in your knitting projects. Colors are not carried across the back of your work, but each color is wound up on bobbins. For example if you are knitting a pattern which takes three colors each color is wound up on bobbins before you begin. To know exactly how many bobbins you need take a look at the Intarsia chart and count the maximum number of color changes in a row. This number is how many bobbins you will need for each color.

1	2	3	4	5	6	7	8	9	10	

Bobbins can be purchased in a craft store, or you can make your own out of stiff paper or cardboard. You will need a bobbin for each color change you perform. In this example of a very simple chart design (my chart design skills aren't that great so please bear with me) you can see that in rows 1 to 3 there are five color changes. For these rows you will need two bobbins of green, two bobbins of white, and one bobbin of red. Each time you need a new color you will use a separate bobbin. And each time you change colors the unused color will rest in the row until you come back across the row and need to pick it up again.

Intarsia Knitting Charts

If you are flat knitting an Intarsia chart is read from right to left and left to right. The cast on is not counted as the first row. The first row begins by reading the chart from the bottom right corner and knitting across the row. The second row is read from left to right. An easy way to remember how to read an Intarsia chart is the odd rows are read from right to left, and the even rows are read from left to right.

If you are working in the round you will read each row from right to left since you never turn your work unless the pattern tells you to. You work color changes in the same manner; the only difference is reading the chart in one direction only.

Color Changes in Intarsia Knitting

You perform color changes like any other knitting project. Drop the old color and start to knit with the new color. Capture the old color in the new stitch by pulling it in front of the new color yarn. Pulling the old color in front of the new yarn on the wrong side and knitting the next stitch will give you a straight line in the pattern. If you need to slant the edges to the left then you will need to twist the yarn on the wrong side of the fabric, while a right slant is twisted on the right side of the fabric. This might sound a bit confusing, but once you start to work with the yarn and colors it will all come together.

Controlling the Yarn Bobbins

One of the most challenging things about Intarsia knitting is keeping the bobbins from tangling. As you turn your work you will need to be very careful to keep the yarn straight and not let it twist up. A few suggestions for you are to use empty toilet paper rolls as bobbins and a large dowel. Wind the yarn you need on toilet paper rolls, prop a dowel between two chairs, and then slip the bobbins onto the dowel. This helps keep the bobbins from twisting and gives you a steady supply of yarn. Another suggestion is to use a coffee can with a lid. Poke holes into the lid for each color of yarn and place the bobbins in the can. Thread the yarn through the lid and use the colors this way.

Here is an example of very pretty Intarsia sweater. All of the color changes were done by using yarn wound up on bobbins. As the color changed the old color was dropped and the new color picked up. As the artist worked across the rows the unused colors rested in place until needed again when she worked back across the row.

Fair Isle Color Technique

Fair Isle knitting is an age old technique which creates beautiful and intricate designs in your knitting. Unlike Intarsia where colors are picked up and dropped as needed, in Fair Isle colors are carried across the back of your knitting. This stranding technique enables you to make several color changes quickly and results in some of the most stunning knitting projects you will see.

Unlike Intarsia where many colors may be used in one row, with Fair Isle only two colors per row are used since the unused colors are carried along the back of the fabric. In the example you can see there are many colors used in the fabric, but if you look closely you will see there are only two colors used per row.

Color Changes in Fair Isle

You knit color changes in Fair Isle by picking up the new color and completing the stitch. The old color is captured under the yarn over of the new color. The colors are not dropped, but "floated" along the back of your fabric. For example on a knit row the colors are floated on the wrong side. When you turn your work and you are knitting the purl row the color floats will now be facing you since the wrong side of the fabric is now facing you. So always remember to float the colors on the purl side of the fabric. This is true if you are flat knitting or knitting in the round.

Notice in this example of a stocking how the colors are captured and floated between the stitches. When you yarn over with the new color capture the old color underneath for knit, and on top for purl to capture and float the old color along the row. You do not break the yarn nor do you let the old colors rest in the row. Here is the finished stocking so you can compare the wrong side with the right side.

Fair Isle Charts

Fair Isle charts are read like any other knitting chart. When flat knitting start at the bottom right corner and read the odd rows from right to left, and the even rows from left to right. When you are knitting in the round you would read each row from right to left since the right side of the fabric is always facing you. Use a highlighter or placeholder of some sort to help you keep track of which row you are on. Charts are usually numbered making it easier to track your progress as you knit.

Fair Isle Chart Examples

In this example of a Fair Isle chart you can see that there are no graph lines to tell you how many stitches you will need to work. Find the widest section of the pattern and count the stitches. This gives you the number of stitches across the widest part of the pattern. Now you will need to figure out how many stitches you want as a border. Divide this number by two and this will give you the number of stitch you need to add to the widest section of the pattern. For each row write then number of stitch on each side of the pattern to equal the number of stitches to make the pattern square.

For example the longest row has 40 stitches and you want a border of 10 stitches on each side. This brings the stitch count for the longest row to 60. Using row 3 as an example the pattern has 8 stitches. Subtract this number from 60 and you have 52 stitches. Each side of the pattern will need to have 26 stitches to make the pattern square. Row 4 has 10 stitches to each side will need 25 stitches to make it square and so on. Yes there is some math involved, but it is simple if you take it row by row.

The following chart is an example of a pattern repeat. Simply work the pattern going back to the beginning of the row until you have knitted the appropriate number of repeats to achieve the size you desire.

Creating Ribbing and Cables

Ribbing is a popular method to add texture and interest to a project. Ribbing is also used to create wristbands, waistbands, and neckbands on garments. Ribbing is stretchy, but helps a garment retain its shape. By combining knit and purl stitches you can create attractive ribbing very easily.

Simple Ribbing

One of the easiest ways to add ribbing is to alternate one knit stitch and one purl stitch. For example if you are flat knitting the pattern repeat would look like this:

Row 1: *Knit 1, purl 1*

Row 2: *Purl 1, knit 1*

The knit stitches on the right side of the fabric would line up with the purl stitches on the wrong and vice versa. This pattern creates a very stretchy fabric and is popular for banding on sleeves and waists.

However remember that when you are knitting in the round the right side is always facing you so the pattern would repeat knit 1, purl 1 on all rows.

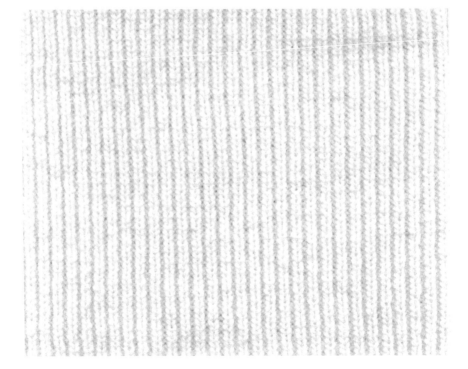

More Defined Ribbing

You can create ribbing of any width by combining and alternating knit and purl stitches. In this example the pattern repeat consists of knit 2, purl 2. This creates a more defined rib. Ribs can be as wide as you desire. Experiment with different widths of ribbing and switch up the number of knit and purl stitches to make swatches you can refer to when you want to add ribbing to your next project.

Cables

Cables are a fun way to add interest, design, and texture to a project. You may be familiar with Aran Fisherman's sweaters which feature intricate and stunning cable designs. These sweaters are one color, but the cables and ribbing make them works of art. Cables may look complicated, but once you understand how they are formed and how to read a cable chart you'll be adding them to your projects in no time.

Cable Charts

Most projects which use cables use chart patterns. These are read like any other chart, but the cable section takes a bit of understanding to knit properly. A cable has a dominate leg. The leg of the cable which is on top is the dominate one. These legs switch places as the cable winds its way up the fabric. Sometimes the legs will vary in width and you can even use different colors for the legs to add a dramatic effect.

When you look at the cable chart you can see how many stitches are in each leg, and which leg is dominate. The charts will also tell you the stitches you need to use to knit each cable. For example the first two cable charts use one stitch for the dominate leg and two for the leg below. To knit the first example slip one stitch onto the cable needle and hold it to the back of your work. Knit 2 and then purl 1 off of the cable needle. When you come back across the row you will then slip 2 stitches onto the cable needle, purl 1 and then knit 2 stitches from the cable needle.

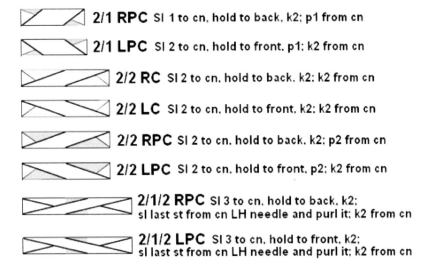

How to Knit a Cable

In the following example you can see how the cables have one leg which has three stitches, and one leg has two stitches. The legs alternate to form the cable pattern in the knitted fabric. The fabric around the cables is knitted in the purl stitch while the cables themselves are knitted with the knit stitch. This adds another dimension of texture and depth to the fabric.

At the point at which the first cables cross (working right to left) slip three stitches onto a cable needle and hold these stitches on the front of your fabric. Knit the next two stitches and then knit the three stitches off of the cable needle. At the next cable crossing you would slip two stitches onto a cable needle and hold them to the back of the fabric and knit three stitches. Now knit the stitches off of the cable needle and you've formed the second cable.

How you hold the stitches on the cable needle will determine if the leg will be on top or underneath. If you want the leg to be on top, hold the stitches on the cable needle on the right side of the fabric (toward you). If you want the leg to be underneath the dominate leg, hold the stitches on the cable needle on the back of the fabric (away from you) while you knit the other leg. When you turn your work you will work the cable stitches in the opposite manner so that they will stay uniform.

Cable Increases and Decreases

The most interesting patterns can be achieved with cable increases and decreases. The increase or decrease is always knitted on the underside cable to hide the stitches. So if you have a cable in which you need to increase or decrease the stitches you would knit the increase or decrease on the leg of the cable which will be hidden. This may be on the cable needle or the knitting needles depending on which leg of the cable will be underneath the dominate one. Here is an example of a cable chart with increases and decreases.

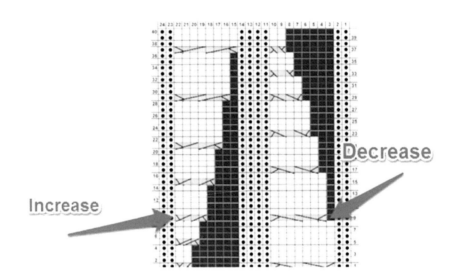

Intermediate Knitting Techniques

In this chapter we'll cover some intermediate knitting techniques to make your life easier and help to advance your knitting skills. In the back of this book I've included links to helpful videos to illustrate the techniques in detail.

Steeking

Steeking refers to cutting knitted fabric. Now I know what you're thinking, "if I cut my knitted fabric it will unravel!" Well yes, but if done correctly you can cut knitted fabric safely without worry of it unravelling and your project being ruined. Why would you want to cut knitted fabric in the first place? Steeking is used mainly in Fair Isle work to add sleeves and other elements to a tube of knitted fabric. Since most Fair Isle patterns are pretty complicated it is easier to add armholes for sleeves after the main body of the sweater is knitted. It is also used to open up a tube of knitted fabric to create a cardigan and add a zipper or button placket.

First take a look at the stitches in the fabric. See the "v" of the knitted stitches and the loop between them? It is this loop we will cut. But first we must make sure the stitches are secure. How we do this is to crochet a line of stitches vertically into the fabric on both sides of where we want to cut.

Make a slip knot and place it on the crochet hook. Insert the hook into the space between the stitch we will cut and the next stitch. Yarn over the hook and pull the yarn through the fabric and through the slip knot on the hook. Insert the hook into the next stitch directly below the first one, yarn over the hook, pull through the fabric and through the loop on the hook. Repeat this process working your way down the fabric in a straight line using the columns of stitches as your guide. When you reach the end of the fabric pull the yarn through the loop on the hook and cut it leaving a long tail. Turn the fabric over and repeat the process on the other side of the fabric until you have two lines of crochet with one complete stitch between them.

With sharp shears cut between the "v" of the center stitch. You may want to pull the fabric apart just a bit to reveal the inner loop of the "v" stitch. Carefully cut up the column of the stitch. When you finish the edges of the steek will curl under a bit, but that is normal. Leave the crochet stitches in the fabric to secure the stitches and now you're ready continue with the project. (You may want to use the same color yarn to crochet with so that the steek does not show.)

You may now sew on sleeves, pick up the stitches on the edge of the steek and knit on an addition to the fabric, or you can just leave the steek as is. If the yarn is animal fibers the steek will naturally felt as time goes on and become more secure. If you've crocheted correctly the steek is now secure and the fabric will not unravel.

Crochet up the side of the stitches to secure.

Crochet the other side in the same manner.

Cut the steek.

Lifelines

Lifelines are an essential part of intermediate and advanced knitting. They save you many hours of headache and your sanity if you have to rip part of your project out. For example if you are knitting along and find out you made a mistake and need to rip out part of your project you may or may not be able to figure out where you are in the pattern once you have ripped out that section. With a lifeline you can easily count the rows and pinpoint exactly where in your pattern you are once you rip out the section you need to.

Lifelines are nothing more than a contrasting color of yarn woven into your knitting. Thread a tapestry needle with a contrasting color of yarn and carefully weave it into the row. Mark on your pattern which row you wove the lifeline into, and as you work the pattern move the lifeline and mark your pattern. This simple and easy habit will then make your life much easier when you make a mistake and have to backtrack in the pattern.

Joining Yarn

There will be times when you are knitting when you need to join yarn. There are two methods to seamlessly join yarn. One is called the spit splice and the other is the Russian join. Both work well and let you continue knitting without breaking the yarn and adding a new strand to your work.

Spit Splicing

As the name implies spit splicing uses spit to join yarn. This method can only be used for animal fibers. It will not work with synthetic or plant fiber yarns since they will not felt. The protein found in your saliva combined with the friction of rubbing your hands together felts the fibers together and creates a strong bond.

First fray the ends of the yarn. Now lick the palm of your hands and place the yarns in one palm so the ends overlap. Rub the palms of your hands together vigorously to cause friction and heat. Keep rubbing until the two pieces of yarn become one. You may have to lick your palms again and really get into it and rub your palms together. This creates a strong bond between the pieces of yarn which is permanent and almost seamless. You may notice a bit of thickness at the join, but unless you know it is there you won't be able to see it.

Russian Join

The Russian join can be used on all types of yarn fibers. The join creates a bit of thickness so very bulky yarns may not work well with this type of join. With the first piece of yarn thread a tapestry needle. Pull a fairly long tail up through the needle. Now you will be weaving the needle back onto the thread and creating a loop. Start weaving the yarn about ½ inch from the needle and weave it back and forth through the yarn fibers for about an inch. Pull the yarn through the needle and thread the second piece of yarn into the tapestry needle.

Insert the tapestry needle into the loop formed by the first piece of yarn and sew the yarn back onto itself just like you did with the first piece of yarn. Remove the needle and grasp the two pieces of yarn, one in each hand, and tug gently. The stitches in the yarn will tighten and join the yarns to create a tight bond. Smooth the new joined piece of yarn with your hand and you're read to keep knitting.

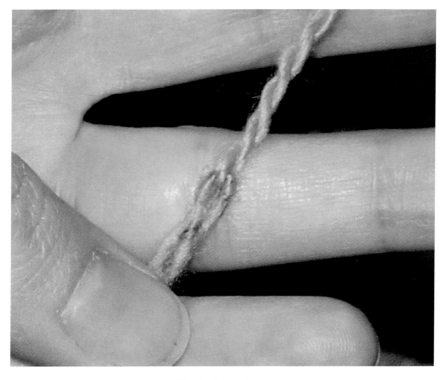

Russian Join method

Thank you for purchasing this book on intermediate knitting. My goal for this book was to introduce you to some of the techniques you can use to advance your knitting skills. There's always something to learn so be sure to check out the links to the videos I've provided at the end of this book, and use them as starting points to explore the craft and art of knitting even further. I hope my book has helped you and that you are encouraged to continue on this wonderful journey in knitting. Thanks again and all my best!

Dorothy

Video Links

Reading Charts
https://www.youtube.com/watch?v=LJBO6PzQeTc
Very Pink Knits

Introduction to Intarsia Knitting
https://www.youtube.com/watch?v=I7G4yzCzpHk
Knit Picks

Learn to Knit Fair Isle Part 1
https://www.youtube.com/watch?v=RNtnTcE7Qjs
Very Pink Knits

Learn to Knit Fair Isle Part 2
https://www.youtube.com/watch?v=2Iv7t63knOA
Very Pink Knits

Learn to Knit Fair Isle Part 3
https://www.youtube.com/watch?v=MvFcq66qco4
Very Pink Knits

How to Cable for Beginners
https://www.youtube.com/watch?v=Ttb_21O6xZ0
Knit Picks

Advanced Cable Techniques: Increasing & Decreasing Cables
https://www.youtube.com/watch?v=W8His4vTd4s
Knit Picks

Knit Picks Advanced Cabling Techniques: Intarsia Cables
https://www.youtube.com/watch?v=h5T943GkwDk
Knit Picks

Steeking
https://www.youtube.com/watch?v=Vno-cMURQjc
Very Pink Knits

Lifelines
https://www.youtube.com/watch?v=ae7pobnLKGQ
Very Pink Knits

Spit Splicing
https://www.youtube.com/watch?v=8uLiFOVmcUU
Very Pink Knits

Russian Join
https://www.youtube.com/watch?v=qWrh8VmTJug
Very Pink Knits

Image Attributions

Intarsia Sweater Back
https://www.flickr.com/photos/milele/2160153342
Image shared on Flickr by Lisa Dusseault

Intarsia Sweater Front
https://www.flickr.com/photos/milele/2160153132
Image shared on Flickr by Lisa Dusseault

Fair Isle Fabric Example
https://www.flickr.com/photos/18581265@N05/4218595995
Image shared on Flickr by Diane Wellman

Fair Isle Stocking Wrong Side
https://www.flickr.com/photos/lydialark/8044477548
Image shared on Flickr by Ikonstandski

Fair Isle Stocking Right Side
https://www.flickr.com/photos/lydialark/8044508306
Image shared on Flickr by Ikonstandski

Cable Chart Examples
http://www.jjsknittingknook.com/faq/index.php?p=default&cat=2
Image from JJS Knitting Knook

Increase and Decrease Cable Chart
https://www.youtube.com/watch?v=W8His4vTd4s
Image from Knit Picks video

Steek Right Side
https://www.youtube.com/watch?v=Vno-cMURQjc
Very Pink Knits Knitting Help: Steeking video at 2:00

Steek Left Side
https://www.youtube.com/watch?v=Vno-cMURQjc
Very Pink Knits Knitting Help: Steeking video at 6:11

Lifeline
https://www.flickr.com/photos/67146024@N00/1393830660
Image shared on Flickr by rmkoske

Russian Join
https://www.flickr.com/photos/noricum/331573520
Image shared on Flickr by norikum

Book 3

Expert Knitting

Tips and Techniques to Bring Your Knitting Skills to the Expert Level

By Dorothy Wilks

Thank you for purchasing this book on Expert Knitting. This book is for the advanced knitter who wants
to take their skills to the next level. In this volume we'll cover techniques such as short rows and
provisional cast on. We will also learn about double knitting and Entrelac techniques. It is my goal to
introduce you to some expert knitting techniques to help you explore this wonderful art. So if you're
ready let's get busy!

Contents

Expert Techniques

In this chapter we will go over some expert techniques to help you gain more confidence and skills in knitting. These are techniques you can use to make your knitting more professional and make your projects easier to work. I have included links to videos at the end of this book for you to watch so that you can practice the techniques covered in this chapter.

Continental versus English Style Knitting

If you're like me you learned how to knit by using the English style of knitting. This method is also called throwing. The yarn is held in the right hand and you use your right hand to wrap the yarn around the needles as you knit and purl. While this style is perfectly fine, you may want to try the Continental style of knitting, also known as picking.

The Continental style differs from the English style in a few ways. The yarn is held in the right hand and you don't use your hand to wrap the yarn, instead the needles pick up the yarn from the left hand when knitting the stitches. Many knitters find the Continental style much faster and easier on the hands then the English method.

To hold the yarn bring it up from the palm of your left hand between the pinky and the ring finger. Wrap the yarn over the under your ring, middle fingers, and over your index finger. As you knit the stitches you will use your pinky and ring finger to adjust the tension. You will also use your index finger to control the yarn for knit and purl stitches as well as keeping the stitches from falling off the left needle. Your right hand controls the right needle.

When you need to work a knit stitch insert the right needle knitwise, "pick" the yarn from your index finger on your right hand and complete the stitch. For a purl stitch move the yarn to the front with your index finger and insert the right needle purlwise and "pick" the yarn from your index finger and complete the stitch. As you switch from knit to purl you will pull the yarn to the back or to the front with your index finger.

Once you get used to the Continental method you may find it is faster and easier on your hands than the English method. Both methods are used by knitters of all expertise levels so use the method you find is most comfortable.

Continental Yarn Hold

Continental Knit Stitch

Continental Purl Stitch

Short Rows

Short rows are used for many things in knitting. You use them when knitting Entrelac and you can also use them to create a better fit in a garment. For example if the pattern will be tight in the bust you can use short rows to help add more room in the bust and get a better fit.

Knit to where you want to insert short rows and turn your work. Slip the last stitch you knitted to the left needle. Bring the yarn to the front of the work, slip the stitch back onto the left needle, bring the yarn to the back and slip the stitch back to the right needle. This is called wrapping a stitch. Purl the amount of stitches you need and turn your work. Now you will wrap the first stitch. Pull the yarn forward, slip the first stitch onto the right needle, pull the yarn to the back and slip the stitch back to the left needle and knit the appropriate number of stitches.

When you come to the wrapped stitch slip at the end of the row slip the needle into both the wrap and the next stitch and knit them together. Knit across the row. Turn your work and purl. When you get to the wrapped purl stitch slip the wrap onto the left needle and purl both the wrap and the next purl stitch together. This hides the wrap and makes it invisible on the right side. Continue to purl across the row and continue with the pattern.

Easy Buttonholes

This method of buttonholes is very easy and creates a strong buttonhole. The first step is to reinforce the button hole with a wrapped stitch. In the knit row bring the yarn to the front and slip the first stitch to the right needle. Bring the yarn to the back. The next step is to bind off stitches to form the buttonhole. Do a simple bind off by slipping the next stitch to the right needle and slipping the stitch to the right over this stitch. The yarn stays in the same position because you're not knitting a bind off, but just doing a simple bind off. Bind off as many stitches as you need for the buttonhole and slip the last stitch back onto the left needle.

Turn the work to create the top of the buttonhole. You will now be casting on stitches to form the top of the buttonhole. Cast on one more stitch than you bound off. For example if you bound off three stitches you will cast on four. Pull the yarn to the back of the work. Insert the right needle between the first two stitches, wrap the yarn around the right needle, and pull the yarn through these stitches. Slip this cast on stitch onto the left needle. Before you tighten up the stitch insert the right needle between the first two stitches. Now you can tighten up the first cast on stitch. Wrap the yarn around the right needle and pull the yarn through the stitches with your right needle and slip the cast on stitch onto the left needle.

Continue to cast on as many stitches as you need. After you cast off the last stitch turn the work. Pull the yarn to the back of the work and slip the first stitch to the right needle. Now slip the last cast on stitch on the right needle over the stitch you just slipped onto the right needle. Continue to knit the rest of the row according to your pattern. Now you have a strong and easy buttonhole.

Cables without a Cable Needle

Creating cables without a cable needle is not for the faint hearted. Well actually it's not that hard if you are creating small cables. What you are doing is crossing the stitches before you work them. For example if you are working a cable in which the knit stitches will be crossed in the back (2 knit stitches in back, 1 purl stitch in front) insert the left needle into the third stitch (the purl stitch) and gently pull it over the knit stitches letting them slip off the left needle. Slip the two knit stitch back onto the left needle, slip the purl stitch back onto the left needle, and then you can purl one and knit two creating a crossed cable.

To create the next leg of the crossed cable you will insert the needle into second and third stitch on the left needle knitwise (the two knit stitches) and pull them over the purl stitch letting the purl stitch slip off the needle. Slip the purl stitch back onto the left needle and slip the two knit stitches back onto the left needle. Now you can knit two stitches and purl one forming the next leg of the crossed cable.

Try not to move your work around when the stitches are not on a needle. This method works best when you only have a few stitches to cross. Larger crossed cables require a cable needle so that you don't lose stitches.

How to Pick Up and Knit Stitches

Sometimes it is helpful to add stitches to the side or ends of your knitting. This is a really handy technique to use when you need to add something like a collar or a button placket. Simply insert the right needle under the stitch on the edge and wrap the yarn knitwise and pull it through the stitch. Insert the needle into the next stitch, wrap the yarn knitwise and pull it through onto your needle. Continue to do this until you have added as many stitches as you need. Turn the work and start to knit.

Be sure to catch two loops over the needle when picking up stitches. This creates a strong stitch that will not stretch out and form a hole in your work. You can also use this method to add stitches to the side of a project or anywhere you need to add stitches.

Provisional (Invisible) Cast On

A provisional cast lets you knit in two directions. When creating a provisional cast on use either cotton or acrylic yarn as the provisional yarn so that it does not felt into your work. First knot the two yarns together. Hold the two yarns like you were going to do a long tail cast on. The working yarn should be toward you and the provisional yarn away from you.

Slide the needle under the working yarn, up and under both yarns, and under the working yarn again forming a cast on stitch. The working yarn will form the cast on stitches while the provisional yarn will be carried under the cast on stitches. When you are ready to knit leave the provisional yarn alone and only work with the working yarn.

When you are ready to work on the provisional cast on slide the needle into all of the loops of the working yarn. Once they are all on your needle you can undo the knot and separate the two yarns. Gently pull the provisional yarn out of the cast on stitches being careful not to let any of the cast on stitches fall off of your needle. If they do very carefully slide them back onto your needle. Now you are ready to start knitting from the other direction of the original cast on.

Slide the needle under the working yarn and then up and under both yarns.

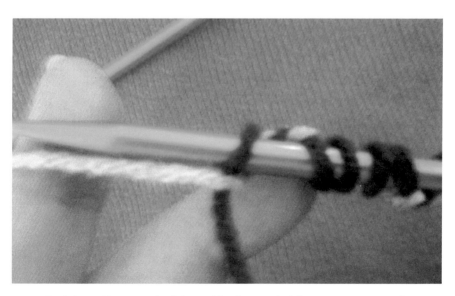

Catch the working yarn and pull the provisional yarn to the left to create a cast on stitch.

A completed provisional cast on

Notice how the provisional yarn is resting in the working yarn's cast on stitches.

Begin by sliding the needle into the cast on loops and then gently removing the provisional yarn. Normally you would bind off the first section of the knitted project but I left the needle in to take this picture. If you're not ready to bind off the first section thread a tapestry needle with contrasting yarn and thread it through the loops on the needle. Remove the needle and you can then work on your project and come back to this end and add more knitting.

Double Knitting

Double knitting creates a fabric with the colors reversed on each side. The fabric is very warm because you are actually knitting two fabrics together. Double knitting may look complicated, but it is really very easy for the advanced knitter to accomplish.

The first step is to cast on the yarn. Select two colors of yarn to use and hold them together as you cast them both onto the needle. Try not to let the colors twist, but if they do this is easily fixed later. Count both strands of yarn as one stitch. For example if your project calls for 20 stitches there will actually be 40 stitches on the needle; 20 of Color A and 20 of Color B.

Once you have the appropriate number of stitches cast onto your needle knit the first two strands together with both strands of yarn. (You will knit the first two and the last two strands together for each row.) Knit the first stitch of Color A with Color A, pull both strands of yarn to the front of the work and purl Color B with Color B. Pull both strands to the back of the work and knit Color A with Color A, pull both strands of yarn to the front of your work and purl Color B with Color B. Continue across the row and then you get to the last set of stitches pull both strands to the back of the work and knit the Both Color A and B with both strands of yarn.

Turn your work and knit the first two strands together with both strands of yarn. Pull both strands to the front and purl Color A with Color A, pull both strands to the back and knit Color B with Color B. Continue across the row and knit the last two stitches together using both strands of yarn.

Here is what to remember about double knitting. Knit stitches will show up on the side of the fabric facing you, and purl stitches show up on the side of the fabric facing away from you. As long as you can keep straight which color is being used to show up on the side of the fabric facing you, you can double knit.

By knitting the first and last sets of stitches together you naturally form a border around your project. If the cast on stitches become twisted slip the correct color over the other stitch, or slip the two stitches off the needle and carefully turn them and slip them back onto your needle.

Color changes are easy. For example if you are using aran and orchid and you've been knitting the orchid, but you need to have a section of aran simply knit the aran stitches and purl the orchid. You can find many charts for double knitting and create very pretty projects with this technique. Scarves and hats made with double knitting are very warm and reversible. The projects end up thick and very spongy which make them perfect for cold weather projects. You can use this technique to knit up reversible bags, hats, garments, socks, kitchen accessories, and décor accessories.

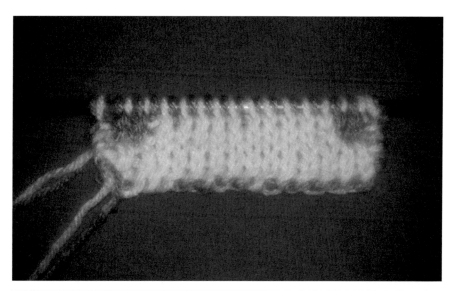

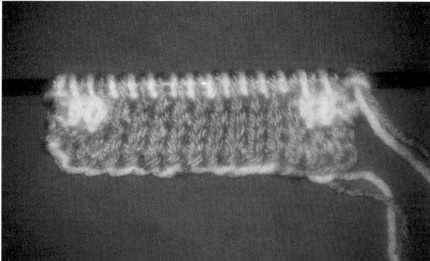

Notice that both sides of the project look like the right side. No purl stitches show and each side is a mirror image of the other one.

Entrelac Knitting

Entrelac knitting creates a beautiful fabric which looks much harder to knit than it actually is. It is a really impressive and stunning project. Entrelac is derived from the French word meaning interlocked. As you knit the levels the triangles and rectangles "interlock" with each other and form a very pretty pattern. You can use just one color, two or as many colors as you like, or use a long strand variegated yarn for a really stunning effect.

Think in Tiers not Rows

Unlike other knitting methods you will not be working all of the way across the row. Instead you'll be doing sets of short rows to begin and then picking up stitches along the sides of the tier below to form the next tier. I know, sounds confusing, but believe me once it clicks you'll find this is a really fun knitting technique. One of the coolest things about Entrelac is the very last tier binds off as you work it. So when you get to your last triangle and purl the stitches together you're done except for the dreaded tails.

First you knit the starting tier, then the right side triangles and rectangles, and then the wrong side triangles and rectangles. You bind off on the wrong side, so you have to plan your tiers accordingly when planning your projects.

Starting Tier (Wrong Side)

Entrelac can use almost any number of base stitches. Let's use 5 and cast on 20 stitches. I prefer the long tail cast on, but use your favorite method and cast on 20 stitches. Now remember we won't be working across all 20 stitches at once.

Row 1: P2, turn (Wrong Side)

Row 1 K2, turn

Row 3: P3, turn

Row 4: K3, turn

Row 5: P4, turn

Row 6: K4, turn

Row 7: P5, do not turn

After finish the first seven rows continue on across to the next stitches working short rows to form the next triangle. Repeat Rows 1 through 7 until you have five sets of triangles. They will look kind of wonky and strange on your needle, but this is how they are supposed to look.

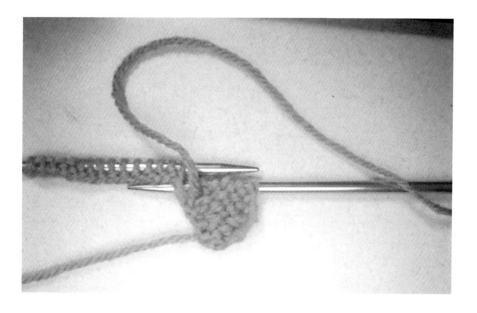

First seven rows forms the first triangle

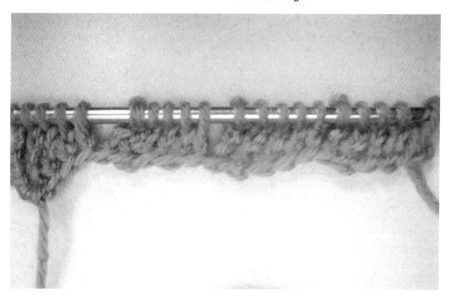

The first tier of triangles completed (they look weird don't they?)

Second Tier (Right Side)

The second tier starts on the right side of the fabric. First you need to work the right side triangle. Each time you start a right side tier you will start with a right side triangle.

Row 1: K2, turn

Row 2: P2, turn

Row 3: KFB (knit into the front and back of the first stitch) SSK (slip, slip, knit). This joins the right side triangle with the triangle or rectangle on the needle. Turn

Row 4: Purl stitches just knit

Row 5: KFB, K1, SSK, turn

Row 6: Purl stitches just knit

Row 7: KFB, K2, SSK, do not turn.

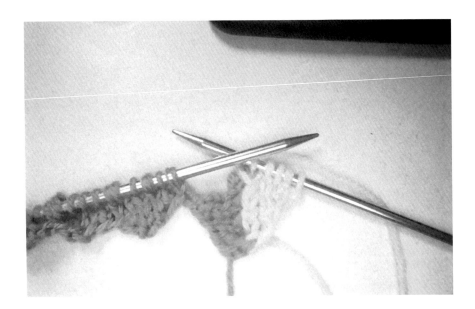

Now the right side triangle is completed and we're ready to move onto the right side rectangles.

First pick up five stitches on the side of the first tier triangle. You will do this every time you start a new rectangle.

Row 1: Pick up and knit 5 stitches along the triangle/rectangle below (insert the needle from the front and wrap the yarn as if to knit and pull through the stitch, turn

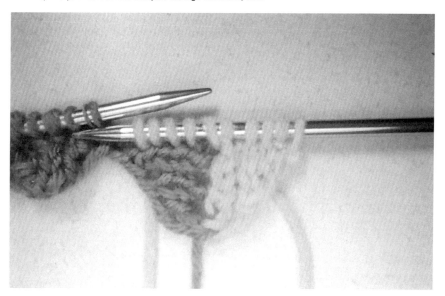

Pick up five stitches from the adjoining triangle or rectangle

Row 2: P5, turn

Row 3: Sl 1 st, K3, SSK, turn (Do not turn on the last row)

Repeat Rows 2 and 3 slipping the first knit stitch and knitting to the last stitch and then slip, slip, and knit to join the rectangle to the triangle or rectangle in the tier below. Each knit row will use one more stitch from the adjoining triangle or rectangle. You only purl the stitches you have knit in the previous row, not all of the way across the row. By slipping the first knit stitch you form a nice even edge to pick up stitches on when you work the next tier. You can knit the first stitch if you like, either way is correct. You may also want to slip the first stitch knitwise and the second stitch purlwise. This seems to make the decrease look smoother, but it's up to you.

Once you have used all of the stitches in the previous tier's triangle or rectangle start back at Row1 and work across the row beginning each new rectangle by picking up five stitches on the side of the previous tier's triangles or rectangles.

Left Side Triangles

When you reach the end of the second tier you must then create a left side triangle.

Row 1: Pick up five stitches from the edge of the far left triangle in the previous tier.

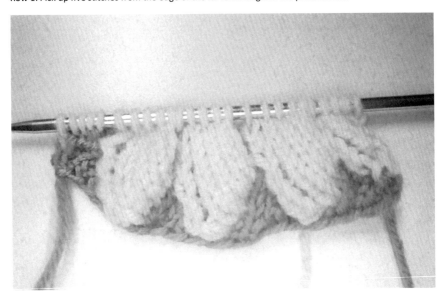

Row 2: P2tog, P3, turn

Row 3: K4, turn

Row 4: P2tog, P2, turn

Row 5: K3, turn

Row 6: P2tog, P1, turn

Row 7: K2, turn

Row 8: P2tog, but do not turn.

You will have one stitch left on your right needle. Now it is time to do the Wrong Side Rectangles and the next tier.

Wrong side of completed tier 2

Row 1: Since you already have one stitch on your right needle you will only need to pick up four stitches to begin the first wrong side rectangle. All other rectangles start with picking up five stitches. Insert the needle from the back of the work and wrap the yarn like you were going to purl.

Row 2: Knit the four picked up stitches and the stitch left on your needle from the previous tier (on subsequent rectangles you will pick up five stitches and knit them), turn

Row 3: Sl st, P3, P2tog to join the rectangle and the adjoining rectangle from the tier below, turn

Repeat Rows 2 and 3 until you have used up all of the stitches from the previous tier's rectangle. Do not turn your work but pick up five stitches on the side of the next adjoining rectangle and work Rows 2 and 3. Do this for each rectangle until you reach the end of the row.

Binding Off

Before you bind off you must work another row of a right side triangle, right side rectangles, and a left side triangle. You can knit as many rows of Entrelac as you want, but you must always end up with a right side tier before you work the bind off row. Binding off is done on the wrong side.

In our bind off tier we will be using six stitches instead of five. This helps the bind off to be smooth and much easier. As you purl the stitches naturally bind themselves off. It's a pretty cool technique.

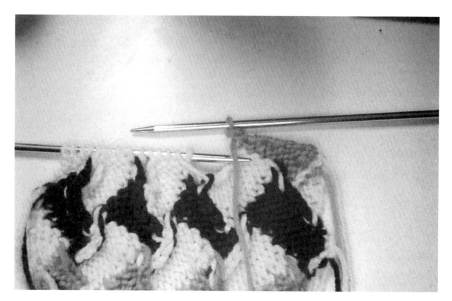

Row 1: Pick up 5 stitches on the purl side. You will have six stitches on your right needle, turn

Row 2: K6, turn

Row 3: P2tog, P3, P2tog (use the picked up stitch and the stitch from the adjoining rectangle to join them just as you did with previous tiers), turn

Row 4: Knit, turn

Row 5: P2tog, P1, P2tog, turn

Row 6: Knit, turn

Row 7: P2tog, P1, P2tog, turn

Row 8: Knit, turn

Row 9: P2tog twice, turn

Row 10: Knit, turn

Row 11: P3tog

Repeat Rows 1 through 11. When you reach the end of the row pull the yarn through and break. Weave in the ends. (You will pick up five stitches for each rectangle in this tier.)

Three Color Entrelac

Two Color Entrelac

You can find lots of free Entrelac patterns online to practice this technique. Entrelac can also be knitting in the round. Be sure to check out the link I provided at the end of this book for an excellent tutorial and a free scarf pattern from the Sapphires and Purls Blog.

End Notes

Thank you so much for purchasing this book. I hope it helps you advance your knitting skills and introduces you to new techniques and methods of enjoying knitting. My mother was a master knitter and created beautiful projects. Her love of knitting spurred my interest in it and I'm still knitting several years later although I'm nowhere near her skill level. Don't be afraid to try new things, it is by challenging ourselves we learn and grow.

All my best,

Dorothy

Video Links

These links are to videos which will help you learn the techniques I have covered in this book. I am a very visual learner and I know it helps me to watch someone actually do the techniques I'm trying to learn. I hope they are valuable companions to this book.

Continental (picking) English (throwing)
https://www.youtube.com/watch?v=XuRLFl36tDY
Craft Sanity

Short Rows
http://www.knittinghelp.com/video/play/short-rows
Knitting Help

Easy Buttonholes
http://www.knittinghelp.com/video/play/buttonhole
Knitting Help

Cables without a Cable Needle
http://www.knittinghelp.com/video/play/crossing-cables-without-a-cable-needle
Knitting Help

How to Pick Up Stitches
http://www.knittinghelp.com/video/play/pick-up-and-knit-stitches
Knitting Help

Provisional (Invisible) Cast On
http://www.knittinghelp.com/video/play/invisible-provisional-cast-on
Knitting Help

Double Knitting
https://www.youtube.com/watch?v=Z0uwla1VYHQ
RJ Knits

Entrelac Knitting Tutorial
http://www.sapphiresnpurls.com/2012/06/entrelac-tutorial.html
Sapphire and Purls

Made in the USA
Middletown, DE
13 December 2016